A

Spelling and Reading

Aid

for Beginners

By

Cheryl .M. Greenidge

First edition 2015

Cover design by Cheryl .M. Greenidge
Edited by E. Jerome Davis
Proofread by Ima Reece
Published by Cheryl .M. Greenidge

ISBN-13: 978-1511972185

ISBN-10: 1511972181

ABOUT THE AUTHOR

Cheryl Greenidge attended St. Martin's Girl's School, the Princess Margaret Secondary School and the Barbados Community College. In 1988, she started her career as a primary school teacher. In 1997, she enrolled at the Erdiston Teacher's Training College where she completed her Diploma in Education. In 2005, Cheryl was made Early Childhood Coordinator at the St. Martin's - Mangrove Primary School. Cheryl's years of experience in the infants' department have greatly assisted her in compiling the material for this book. Cheryl is the author of 'Word Building for Infants' and 'Grammar Made Easy for Infants – Books 1 &2'.

CONTENTS

PREFACE

'A Spelling and Reading Aid for Beginners' consists of a variety of reading, spelling and writing activities which are introduced gradually to reinforce seventy-seven list words. This book is designed to help build confidence in the beginner reader.

'A Spelling and Reading Aid for Beginners' contains reading activities such as matching words that are the same and matching words to pictures and phrases. Writing activities include writing the missing letters, words, phrases and sentences for given pictures. Also included are many word searches which greatly improve word recognition and spelling skills, and are presented with an increasing progression of difficulty.

It is hoped that as a result of using this workbook that solid reading foundation skills will be gained, from which future reading competence can be built.

Part 1

✿ Call the words for the pictures. Match the words
that are the same.

bird

little

boy

bird

girl

big

see

✿ Match the pictures to the words.

see

girl

little

big

bird

boy

3

❀ Look for the words in the lines and circle them.

Example:

boy	k s x b o y l e

see	t s e e w d y a n
big	r k c n b i g u f
girl	o s h g i r l c t
boy	m e b o y l t a s
bird	y t s o g b i r d
little	k s l i t t l e x

✿ Draw the picture for the word.

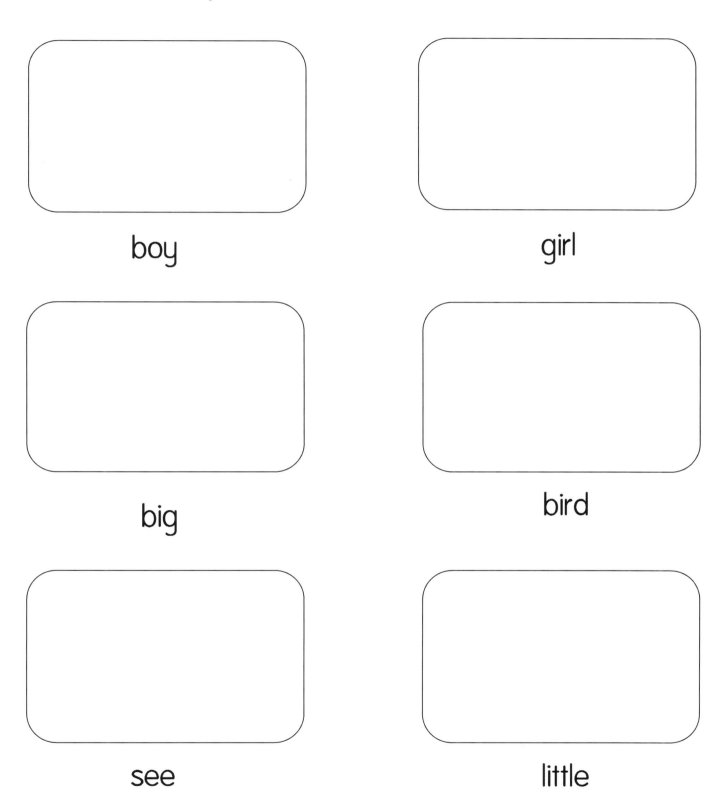

boy

girl

big

bird

see

little

✿ Call the words for the pictures. Match the words that are the same.

man   box

box   one

| one   man

2 two   two

can   tree

tree   can

6

✿ Match the pictures to the words.

2

man

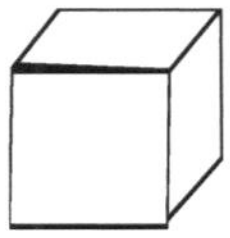

two

box

can

tree

one

✽ Look for the words in the lines and circle them.

tree	s a t r e e h c n
man	c y w m a n o z b
box	f v t r w b o x n
can	u k l c a n x m o
two	e t w o s f h w n
one	p s d c o n e a k

❀ Draw the picture for the word.

box

man

two

tree

can

one

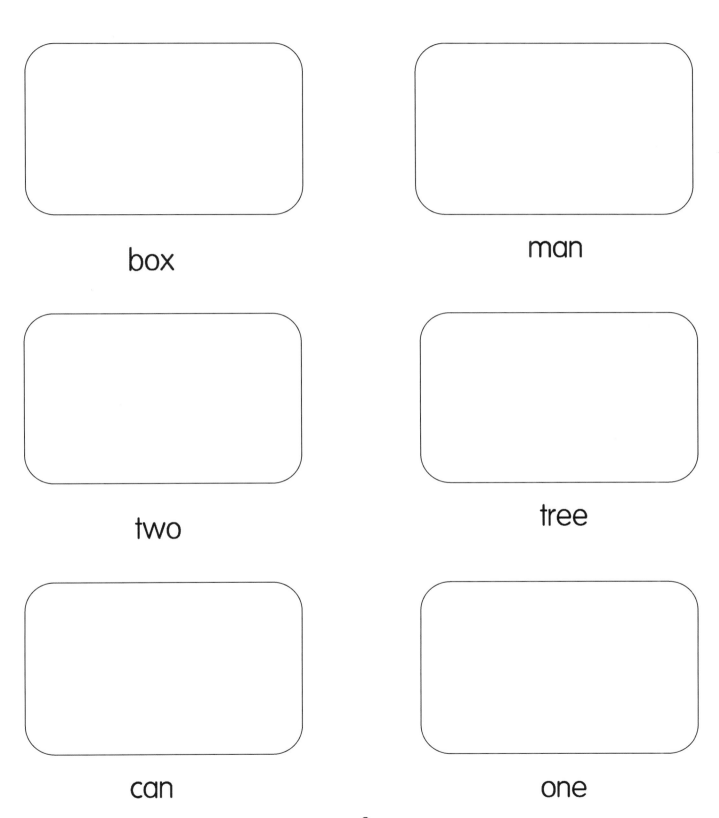

✻ Write the missing letter and copy the word.

__an

_____

__ee

_____

__ox

_____

b__rd

_____

t__ee

_____

b__y

_____

ma__

_____

2

tw__

_____

gir__

_____

10

✿ Look for the words in the lines and circle them.

| and | b w **a n d** g s x n |

| you | m t n g k c **y o u** |

| the | g **t h e** o m r y a |

| look | i h f **l o o k** s x |

| at | b o **a t** f p i b s |

| in | h f g r w o **i n** m |

✿ Write the missing letters and copy the words.

big	see	and	in
the	is	look	at

th__   __nd   __t   __n

_____   _____   _____   _____

__s   s__ __   b__g   l__ __k

_____   _____   _____   _____

✿ Write the word for the picture.

boy	bird	girl	tree

_____   _____   _____   _____

✿ Circle the word for the picture.

2

one

too

two

dig

big

bin

sea

tree

see

con

can

cat

look

like

little

1

one

own

two

✿ **Match the words to the pictures.**

one big girl

two little boys

a boy and a girl

the big man

14

❀ Write the correct words for the pictures.

┌─────────────────────────────┐
│   a boy and a girl   │
└─────────────────────────────┘

┌──────────────────────┐   ┌──────────────────────┐
│ two little boys   │   │   the big man   │
└──────────────────────┘   └──────────────────────┘

15

✤ Match the words to the pictures.

two little girls

a bird and a box

one big girl

the big tree

16

✿ **Write the correct words for the pictures.**

a bird and a box

one big girl

two little girls

✿ **Write the words under the correct boxes.**

the trees	two boys	a bird

one girl	the man	a box

_____

_____

_____

_____

_____

_____

18

✿ Look for the words in the lines and circle them.

is	a y f n o i s p c

come	z l h c o m e g u

it	s f i t v e d f r

that	e c f p t h a t k

she	w i s h e q v h a

to	s c v f g b n t o

❀ Write the missing letters and copy the words.

it	two	you	to
he	one	she	little

tw___   y___u   ___t   ___n___

_____   _____   _____   _____

sh___   t___   h___   l___ttl___

_____   _____   _____   _____

❀ Write the word for the picture.

see	little	one	big

_____   _____   _____   _____

20

❀ Circle the word for the picture.

three

tree

see

bob

bay

boy

men

mane

man

grill

grid

girl

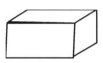

fox

box

bog

bird

girl

dirt

✾ **Look for the words in the lines and circle them.**

he	n i r **h e** s f b m
want	b **w a n t** d a v h
says	b o g r d **s a y s**
please	a **p l e a s e** t u
for	x m **f o r** e t d a
thank	h k o **t h a n k** g

❀ **Write the missing letters and copy the words.**

for	says	come	that
thank	please	can	want

w__nt   s__ys   f__r   th__t

_____   _____   _____   _____

th__nk   c__m__   c__n   pl____s__

_____   _____   _____   _____

❀ **Write the word for the picture.**

can	man	two	box

   **2**

_____   _____   _____   _____

⊛ Find the words and circle them.

s	**g**	**i**	**r**	**l**	p	s	h	x	f
p	k	y	q	w	**t**	**r**	**e**	**e**	k
b	**o**	**x**	z	y	m	z	h	v	c
q	p	s	v	u	u	c	m	l	t
w	b	v	f	h	r	**b**	**o**	**y**	s
m	**a**	**n**	h	w	q	e	k	z	l
p	b	g	r	t	**b**	**i**	**r**	**d**	t
r	u	s	a	n	t	z	c	m	o

girl   tree   box

boy   man   bird

24

✿ **Find the words and circle them. (2a)**

g	i	r	l	a	t	r	e	e	w
f	n	l	k	s	d	p	o	z	x
i	b	o	x	n	i	o	b	o	y
m	a	n	d	h	b	i	r	d	h
b	r	n	c	n	c	n	b	s	u
s	e	e	o	l	i	t	t	l	e
o	p	b	i	g	c	n	y	o	u
r	t	h	e	r	l	o	o	k	r

girl ✓   tree   box   boy

man   bird   see   little

big   you   the   look

✿ Copy the words twice and learn to spell them.

is   at   in   it

_____   _____   _____   _____

_____   _____   _____   _____

to   he   the   she

_____   _____   _____   _____

_____   _____   _____   _____

and   you

_____   _____

_____   _____

✿ **Find the words and circle them. (2b)**

b	o	x	r	t	b	o	y	r	t
i	o	m	a	n	x	g	i	r	l
t	r	e	e	r	s	a	s	a	s
o	y	a	y	h	z	s	e	e	h
b	i	r	d	h	f	d	t	h	e
k	k	l	o	o	k	p	e	k	k
b	i	g	c	n	c	n	y	o	u
r	r	f	s	l	i	t	t	l	e

girl   tree   box   boy

man   bird   see   little

big   you   the   look

27

✿ Copy the words twice and learn to spell them.

see   big   can   one

_____   _____   _____   _____

_____   _____   _____   _____

two   box   boy   man

_____   _____   _____   _____

_____   _____   _____   _____

for   girl

_____   _____

_____   _____

❀ **Find the words and circle them. (3a)**

b	c	o	m	e	w	s	a	y	s
y	u	y	p	l	e	a	s	e	y
t	h	a	t	n	i	s	e	e	o
b	l	g	v	y	w	n	b	g	s
g	f	o	r	z	v	h	s	h	e
h	v	u	w	a	n	t	m	x	s
l	o	o	k	u	s	w	t	o	n
p	l	i	t	t	l	e	p	h	r
r	b	w	d	s	t	h	a	n	k

come	says	please	that
see	for	she	want
look	to	little	thank

29

✿ Write these words correctly.

	Wrong x	Right ✓
	nam	man
	xbo	___
	yob	___
	irdb	___
	erte	___
	iglr	___

✿ **Copy the words twice and learn to spell them.**

tree   bird   says   want

_____   _____   _____   _____

_____   _____   _____   _____

come   look   that   little

_____   _____   _____   _____

_____   _____   _____   _____

please   thank

_____   _____

_____   _____

✤ Write these words correctly.

	Wrong x	Right ✓
	nac	_____
	ese	_____
2	wot	_____
	gib	_____
I	eon	_____
	iltlet	_____

✿ **Circle the correct word in the brackets.**

1. The boy is in the (box   ball   bed).

2. A bird is in the (big   two   tree).

3. He is a big (boy   man   girl).

4. The bird sees the (big   box   boys).

✾ **Write the sentence for the picture.**

The boy is in the box.

A bird is in the tree.

The girl wants the box.

He is a big man.

1._____

2._____

3._____

4._____

✿ **Find the words and circle them. (3b)**

w	f	o	r	x	r	p	s	h	e
r	x	i	a	f	t	o	e	q	m
s	e	e	b	t	h	a	n	k	n
h	q	d	f	b	g	s	a	y	s
k	d	c	o	m	e	l	t	a	f
p	l	e	a	s	e	g	c	z	r
m	g	v	y	w	n	w	a	n	t
t	h	a	t	f	i	y	d	x	h
f	t	e	p	b	l	o	o	k	d
h	l	i	t	t	l	e	d	m	c

come	says	please	that
see	for	she	want
look	to	little	thank

35

✿ Write the missing words to complete the sentences.

1. The _____ sees the big _____ .

2. The _____ is in the _____ .

3. A _____ is in the _____ .

4. The _____ wants the _____ .

❀ **Read the sentences.**

I can see a boy, a girl and a man.

Is the man big? The man is big.

Is the girl little? The girl is little.

Is the boy little? The boy is little.

❀ **Read the sentences.**

You see the bird, the box and the two trees.

That is one bird. It is little.

That is one little box.

One tree is big and one tree is little.

❀ **Read the sentences.**

Come and look at the little bird in the big tree, says the big man. The boy wants the bird.

That bird is for you, says the man to the boy. Thank you, says the boy to the man.

Come and look at the little bird says the little boy to the girl.

Part 2

✿ **Call the words for the pictures. Match the words that are the same.**

on   beach

read   on

beach   read

write   write

sand   play

play   sand

✿ Match the pictures to the words.

write

play

on

sand

read

beach

43

✽ **Copy the words twice and learn to spell them.**

on

beach

knows

likes

_____ _____ _____ _____

_____ _____ _____ _____

him

read

write

sand

_____ _____ _____ _____

_____ _____ _____ _____

this

play

they

has

_____ _____ _____ _____

_____ _____ _____ _____

❀ Find the words and circle them.

w	r	e	a	d	w	w	s	o	n
b	o	m	r	t	h	e	y	r	m
s	a	k	a	n	i	n	t	o	i
a	s	l	i	k	e	s	r	a	s
h	i	m	d	h	o	w	a	n	t
d	f	d	f	w	r	i	t	e	n
s	a	n	d	t	m	l	e	k	k
p	l	a	y	s	e	t	h	i	s
g	t	h	o	b	e	a	c	h	r
r	h	k	n	o	w	s	h	k	h

read   this   him   on

they   want   sand   play

beach   likes   write   knows

✿ **Call the words for the pictures. Match the words that are the same.**

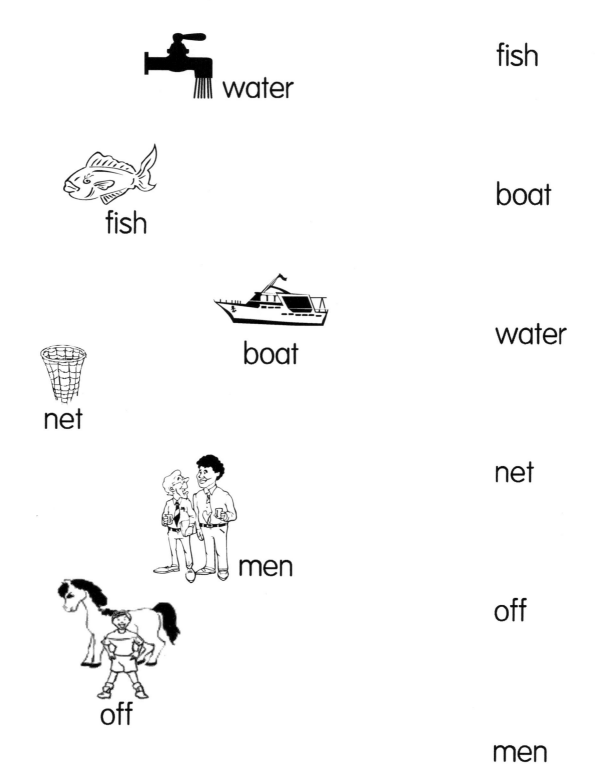

water

fish

fish

boat

boat

water

net

net

men

off

off

men

✿ Match the pictures to the words.

water

net

fish

men

off

boat

47

✿ **Copy the words twice and learn to spell them.**

water   fish   boat   have

_____   _____   _____   _____

_____   _____   _____   _____

nets   men   are   off

_____   _____   _____   _____

_____   _____   _____   _____

go   sea   into

_____   _____   _____

_____   _____   _____

✿ Write the missing letters and copy the words.

kn__ws   l_k_s   h_m   th_s

_____   _____   _____   _____

th__y   h_s   h_v_

_____   _____   _____

✿ Write the word for the picture.

| boat | read | sand | beach |

_____   _____   _____   _____

49

✸ Call the words for the pictures. Match the words
   that are the same.

ball

buy

pull

sea

women

children

buy

ball

women

sea

children

pull

50

✿ **Match the pictures to the words.**

pull

children

ball

women

buy

sea

51

✽ **Find the words and circle them.**

```
t  h  e  y  a  s  n  e  t  s
l  k  u  o  p  i  k  r  d  f
d  q  w  f  i  s  h  b  y  s
r  f  b  n  y  h  a  s  m  a
p  u  l  l  d  x  c  b  n  k
q  s  c  v  g  t  b  o  a  t
h  a  v  e  o  m  e  n  c  x
s  a  f  a  r  e  m  a  c  o
o  t  r  o  f  f  d  f  a  n
s  w  e  r  t  y  s  e  a  l
e  f  w  a  t  e  r  a  d  f
```

pull   are   boat   men

nets   off   have   water

fish   they   sea   has

✿ Write the missing letter and copy the word.

__ead

_____

__rite

_____

__each

_____

p__a__

_____

w__t__r

_____

b__ __t

_____

o__ __

_____

s__n__

_____

f__s__

_____

✿ **Call the words for the pictures. Match the words that are the same.**

eat

mummy

daddy

bag

woman

orange

✿ Match the pictures to the words.

bag

eat

daddy

orange

mummy

woman

55

✿ Copy the words twice and learn to spell them.

pull	with	some	women
_____	_____	_____	_____
_____	_____	_____	_____

buy	ball	woman	mummy
_____	_____	_____	_____
_____	_____	_____	_____

daddy	yes	bag	children
_____	_____	_____	_____
_____	_____	_____	_____

❀ **Write the missing letters and copy the words.**

__r__	g__	__nt__	w__th
_____	_____	_____	_____

s__m__	y__s	w__	__ll
_____	_____	_____	_____

❀ **Write the word for the picture.**

fish	play	write	water

_____   _____   _____   _____

57

�֍ **Copy the words twice and learn to spell them.**

we   eat   all   what

_____   _____   _____   _____

_____   _____   _____   _____

find   no   his   goes

_____   _____   _____   _____

_____   _____   _____   _____

up   me   an   orange

_____   _____   _____   _____

_____   _____   _____   _____

✾ Draw the picture for the word.

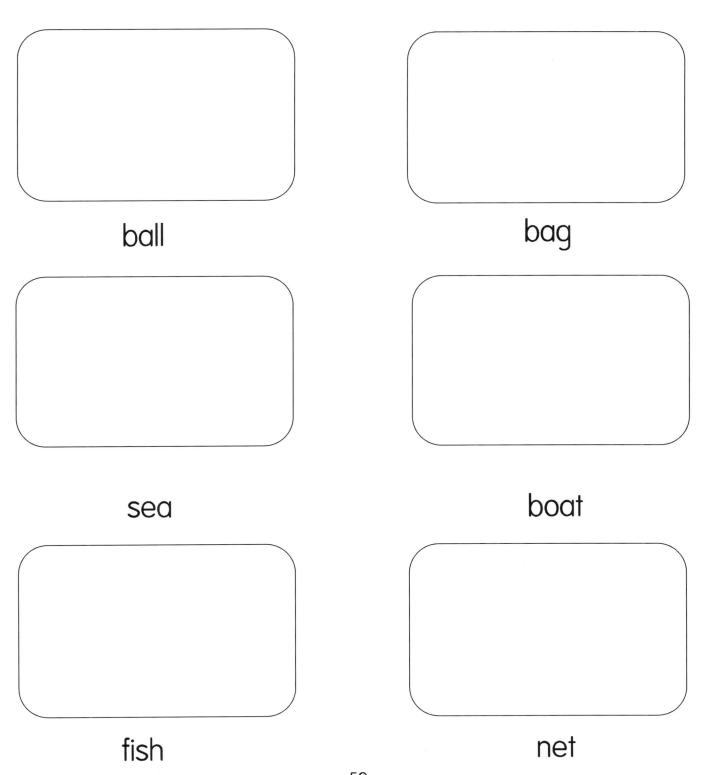

ball

bag

sea

boat

fish

net

59

✿ Write the missing letters and copy the words.

wh__t   f__nd   n__   h__s

_____   _____   _____   _____

g____s   __p   m__   __n

_____   _____   _____   _____

✿ Write the word for the picture.

```
┌─────────────────────────────────────────────────────────┐
   woman          man          men          women
└─────────────────────────────────────────────────────────┘
```

_____   _____   _____   _____

✿ Find the words and circle them.

s	g	o	e	u	i	n	t	o	a
a	s	d	f	g	h	z	k	l	p
s	o	m	e	z	x	w	i	t	h
q	a	w	s	r	d	t	f	y	h
y	y	e	s	l	m	u	m	m	y
p	l	i	k	y	g	t	r	d	e
w	d	r	b	e	a	c	h	g	h
v	b	a	l	l	d	e	s	u	p
d	a	b	l	v	b	u	y	b	n
c	h	i	l	d	r	e	n	z	x
m	g	r	d	t	w	o	m	e	n

women   beach   ball   some

with   go   buy   mummy

children   yes   into   up

61

Circle the word for the picture.

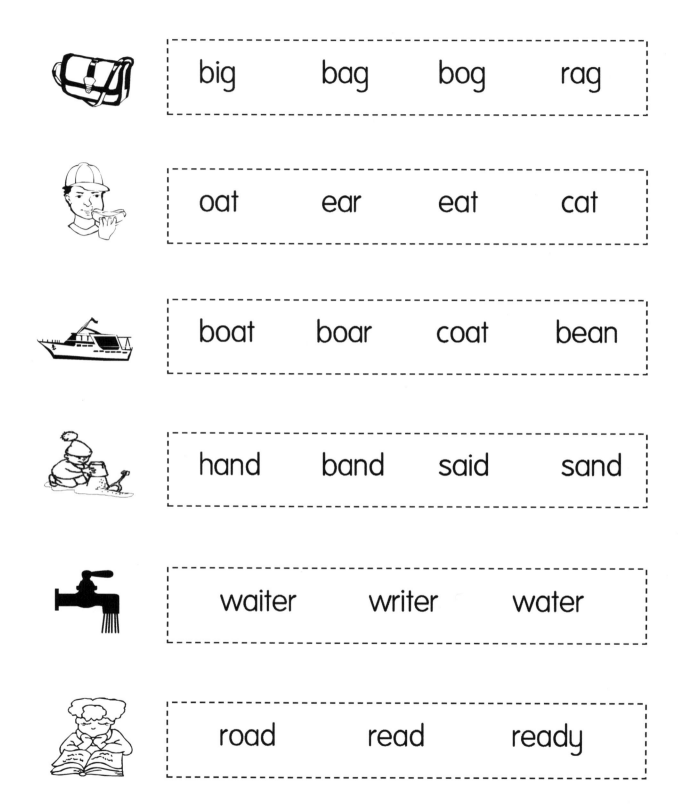

big	bag	bog	rag

oat	ear	eat	cat

boat	boar	coat	bean

hand	band	said	sand

waiter	writer	water

road	read	ready

✿ Find the words and circle them.

d	f	g	h	z	k	b	a	g	c
d	a	d	d	y	s	w	g	m	e
q	s	e	f	b	g	o	e	s	r
w	e	a	a	f	g	h	p	k	r
q	d	w	o	m	a	n	b	t	h
x	z	f	t	o	r	a	n	g	e
v	m	f	g	n	u	o	z	n	o
a	w	h	a	t	o	c	h	i	s
w	f	v	b	n	y	u	m	i	p
x	e	y	w	b	r	f	i	n	d
d	f	e	a	t	m	i	o	p	l

orange	goes	we	daddy
woman	bag	his	eat
find	me	what	no

✿ **Look for the words in the lines and circle them.**

knows	this	goes	beach

c	b	g	r
k	t	s	s
t	h	w	b
d	i	f	e
f	s	t	a
k	n	g	c
n	k	o	h
o	v	e	m
w	d	s	v
s	e	t	d

❋ Circle the word for the picture.

	see	sea	seat	seen

	ten	not	net	met

	dull	pal	put	pull

	water	write	wring

	beach	reach	breach

	range	orange	order

❀ Circle a small word and write it.

the he	that	little
knows	write	sand
this	they	the

Write the missing letter and copy the word.

_ a _

_____

_ ul _

_____

_ a _

_____

d _ dd _

_____

w _ m _ n

_____

m _ m _ y

_____

_ hil _ re _

_____

_ o _ e _

_____

_ r _ n _ e

_____

❀ Find the words and circle them.

s	w	o	s	b	n	n	t	m	r
o	f	w	z	y	o	h	w	f	e
m	b	a	u	w	m	u	h	d	t
e	n	n	a	r	a	a	a	s	h
w	t	t	i	i	h	i	t	f	e
e	h	l	t	t	k	k	f	i	y
r	i	k	h	e	i	f	g	n	e
l	s	e	a	o	k	d	n	d	w
i	k	d	t	m	n	x	w	f	r
k	l	f	c	a	o	c	i	k	e
e	o	r	y	h	w	y	t	l	a
s	p	z	o	k	s	o	h	o	d

some ✓	likes	this	want
that	write	knows	what
with	find	they	read

✿ Circle the word for the picture.

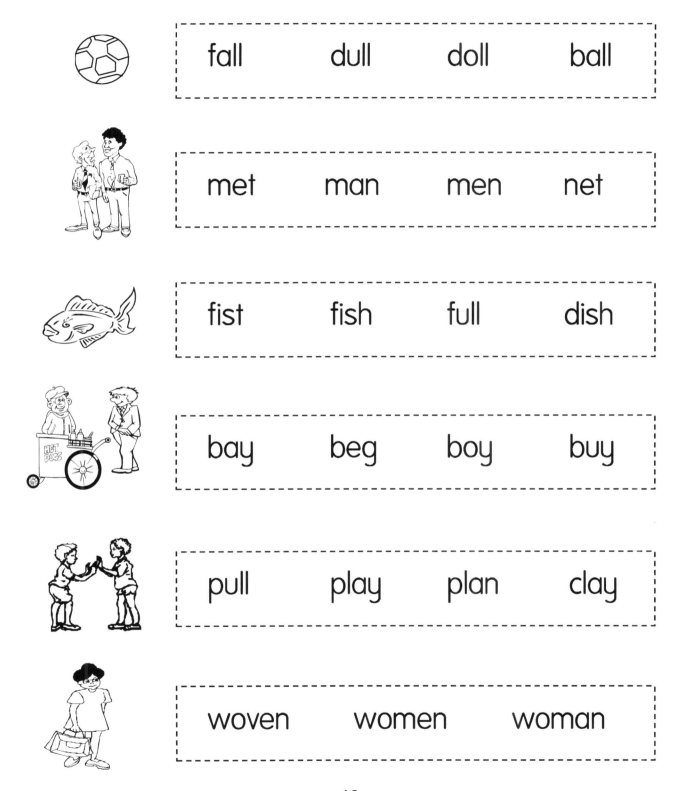

| | fall | dull | doll | ball |

| | met | man | men | net |

| | fist | fish | full | dish |

| | bay | beg | boy | buy |

| | pull | play | plan | clay |

| | woven | women | woman |

69

Circle a small word and write it on the line.

into ____	some ____	ball ____
his ____	what ____	find ____
woman ____	goes ____	orange ____

✿ **Write the sentence for the picture.**

The woman likes to write.

He plays in the sand.

The children like to read.

He has a big fish.

1._____

2._____

3._____

4._____

✿ **Write the missing words to complete the sentences.**

1. The _____ likes to _____ .

2. The _____ buys some _____ .

3. Two _____ are in the _____ .

4. The boys _____ to _____ .

✿ Write these sentences correctly.

box. I a see

1. _____

The little. boy is

2. _____

the at girl. Look

3. _____

bird tree. is the A in

4. _____

man The goes fish. to

5. _____

73

✿ **Write these sentences correctly.**

has bag. a She

1._____

some We water. want

2._____

likes Mummy read. to

3._____

oranges. eat all They the

4._____

The sand. the play children in

5._____

74

Word Lists

Word List 1

is	at	in	it
to	he	the	she
for	you	see	big
can	one	two	box
boy	man	and	girl
tree	bird	says	want
look	come	that	little
	please	thank	

Word List 2

likes	knows	him	read
write	sand	this	play
on	they	water	fish
has	boat	have	nets
men	are	off	go
sea	into	beach	pull
some	with	women	buy
	children	ball	

woman	mummy	daddy	yes
bag	we	eat	all
what	find	no	his
goes	up	me	an

orange

Homework

	Page / Pages		Page / Pages
1		21	
2		22	
3		23	
4		24	
5		25	
6		26	
7		27	
8		28	
9		29	
10		30	
11		31	
12		32	
13		33	
14		34	
15		35	
16		36	
17		37	
18		38	
19		39	
20		40	

Made in the USA
Columbia, SC
05 May 2022